ICONS

CHINA STYLE

CHINA

Exteriors Interiors

STYLE

Details

PHOTOS **Reto Guntli**
EDITOR **Angelika Taschen**

TASCHEN

KÖLN LONDON LOS ANGELES MADRID PARIS TOKYO

Front cover: Far East romance: a concubine's bed in Red Capital Residence.
Couverture: Romance d'Extrême-Orient : lit de concubine au Red Capital Residence.
Umschlagvorderseite: Fernost-Romantik: Das Bett einer Konkubine in der Red Capital Residence.

Back cover: Bright entrance: lantern at Beijing's China Club.
Dos de couverture: Entrée en lumière : lanterne du China Club de Pékin.
Umschlagrückseite: Strahlender Eingang: Eine Laterne im China Club von Peking.

Also available from TASCHEN:

Inside Asia
2 volumes, 880 pages
ISBN-10: 3-8228-1441-5
ISBN-13: 978-3-8228-1441-3

To stay informed about upcoming TASCHEN titles, please request our magazine
at www.taschen.com/magazine or write to TASCHEN, Hohenzollernring 53, D-50672 Cologne,
Germany, contact@taschen.com, Fax: +49-221-254919. We will be happy to send you a free copy
of our magazine which is filled with information about all of our books.

© 2006 TASCHEN GmbH
Hohenzollernring 53, D-50672 Köln
www.taschen.com

Concept and editing by Angelika Taschen, Berlin
Layout and general project management by Stephanie Bischoff, Cologne
Texts by Daisann McLane, New York
Lithography by Horst Neuzner, Cologne
German translation by Christiane Burkhardt/Norbert Pautner, Munich
French translation by Manuel Benguigui for mot.tiff, Paris

Printed in Italy
ISBN-10: 3-8228-4966-9
ISBN-13: 978-3-8228-4966-8

CONTENTS SOMMAIRE INHALT

As recently as 100 years ago, Chinese style was tradition-bound, with aesthetics that reflected the cultural confidence of a country with several thousand years of experience in fine design. Whether it was the curve of the back of a handcrafted Ming chair, or the perfect green glaze of an 800-year-old celadon vase, the elements of high Chinese style seemed set in stone, as unchanging as those of the Great Wall. Chinese decorative objects were the most precious that money could buy, made either of rare natural materials, like jade and hardwoods, or manmade ones, like porcelain, fine paper, and silk, (which, by the way, were all invented in China). Chinese traditional style, of course, still thrives. But, after 1900, with the arrival of Western aesthetics and modernity in China,

LET TEN THOUSAND STYLES BLOOM
Daisann McLane

Il y a encore un siècle, le style chinois était imprégné par la tradition et son esthétique reflétait la confiance d'un pays possédant des milliers d'années d'expérience et de culture artistique. Qu'il s'agisse de la courbe du dossier d'un fauteuil Ming ou du parfait éclat vert d'un vase en céladon vieux de huit cents ans, les éléments du grand style chinois semblaient gravés dans une pierre aussi immuable que celles de la Grande Muraille. Les objets décoratifs chinois étaient les plus précieux au monde, qu'ils soient faits de matériaux naturels rares, comme le jade et les bois exotiques, travaillés, comme la porcelaine, le papier et la soie… autant de matériaux qui, faut-il le rappeler, furent inventés en Chine. Bien entendu, le style traditionnel chinois est toujours vivant. Mais, à partir de 1900, avec l'arrivée de l'esthétique occidentale et de la modernité en Chine, ses horizons se sont élargis. Dans les années 1930, la ville de Shanghai a

Vor nicht einmal 100 Jahren war der chinesische Stil noch äußerst traditionell. In seiner Ästhetik spiegelte sich das kulturelle Selbstbewusstsein eines Landes mit einer jahrtausendelangen Erfahrung in anspruchsvollem Design. Egal, ob es sich um die Rückenlehne eines handgearbeiteten Ming-Stuhls oder die perfekte Seladonglasur einer 800 Jahre alten Vase handelte – die Elemente des gehobenen China-Stils schienen genauso unverrückbar zu sein wie die Chinesische Mauer. Chinesische Deko-Objekte gehörten zum Kostbarsten überhaupt und bestanden entweder aus seltenen Naturmaterialien wie Jade und Harthölzern oder aus Handgemachtem wie Porzellan, Papier und Seide (übrigens alles Dinge, die in China erfunden wurden). Der traditionelle chinesische Stil ist natürlich nach wie vor sehr gefragt. Doch als um 1900 die moderne westliche Ästhetik nach China kam, öffnete sich das Land neuen Stilen. In den 1930er-Jahren

style horizons expanded. In the 1930s, the city of Shanghai embraced Art Deco, while modernism and Soviet monumental architecture entered the picture along with Mao's revolution in 1949. Mao Zedong, who urged the Chinese people to abandon "old ideas, old culture, old customs and old habits," had a profound impact on Chinese style. During the 1960s Cultural Revolution, many of China's most priceless treasures were destroyed. But Mao's rule also left a legacy of mass-produced design and democratic, functional fashion – and a world-famous image that adorns everything Chinese under the sun, ranging from posters, to buttons and teapots. Today, China's restless, creative style-makers are free to play with all periods of their visual heritage, and they do.

embrassé l'Art Déco, tandis que le modernisme et l'architecture monumentale soviétique se sont imposés avec la révolution de Mao en 1949. Mao Zedong, qui pressait le peuple chinois d'abandonner « les vieilles idées, la vieille culture, les vieilles coutumes et les vieilles habitudes », a eu un impact profond sur le style chinois. Ainsi, pendant la Révolution culturelle des années 1960, un grand nombre de trésors inestimables ont été détruits. Toutefois, l'héritage légué par Mao est aussi celui du design de masse et d'une mode démocratique et fonctionnelle – sans oublier ce portrait, connu dans le monde, entier qui orne tous les objets chinois possibles et imaginables, depuis les affiches jusqu'aux boutons de chemise et aux théières.
Aujourd'hui, les designers chinois débordant d'imagination et de créativité sont libres de jouer avec tous les codes visuels de leur héritage, et ils ne s'en privent pas.

begrüßte die Stadt Shanghai begeistert den Art-Deco-Stil, während 1949 im Zuge von Maos Revolution die Moderne sowie die sowjetische Monumentalarchitektur Einzug in China hielten. Mao Zedong, der das chinesische Volk zwang, sich von überholten Ideen, Kulturen, Sitten und Gebräuchen zu trennen, hatte einen enormen Einfluss auf den chinesischen Stil. Während der Kulturrevolution in den 1960er-Jahren wurde ein Großteil von Chinas kostbarsten Schätzen zerstört. Dafür hinterließ Mao massenproduziertes Design und demokratische, funktionale Mode – sowie ein weltberühmtes Konterfei, das jeden nur erdenklichen chinesischen Gegenstand von Postern über Knöpfe bis hin zu Teekannen ziert. Doch heute haben Chinas ebenso umtriebige wie kreative Designer die Freiheit, mit allen Epochen ihres kulturellen Erbes zu spielen – eine Freiheit, von der sie auch reichlich Gebrauch machen.

«...Poverty is not socialism. To be rich is glorious!...»

Deng Xiaoping

«...La pauvreté n'est pas le socialisme. S'enrichir est glorieux!...»

Deng Xiaoping

»...Armut ist nicht Sozialismus. Reich werden ist glorreich!...«

Deng Xiaoping

EXTERIORS

Extérieurs Aussichten

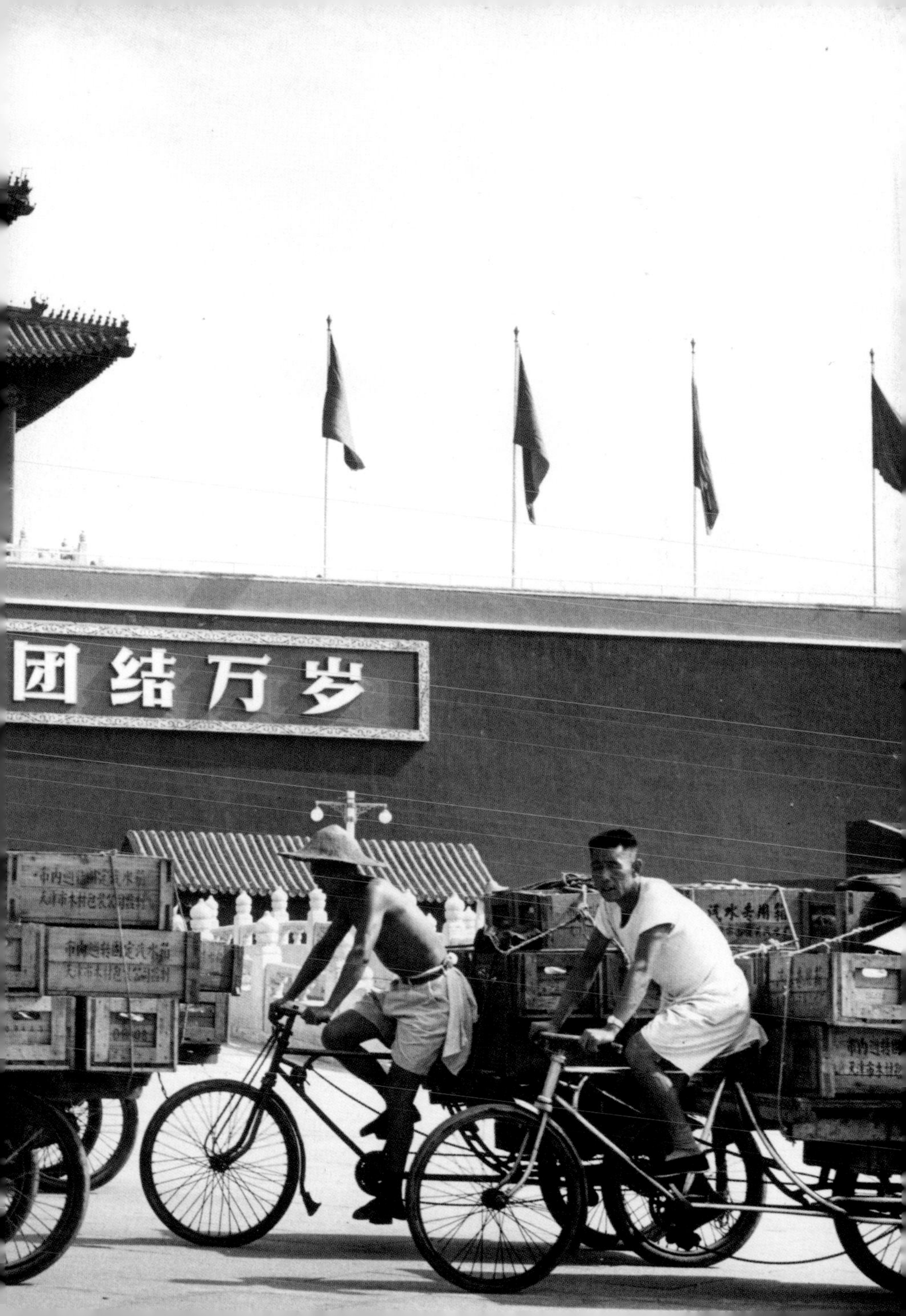
团结万岁

10/11 Nanking Road in downtown Shanghai, 1930. *Nanking Road dans le centre de Shanghai, 1930.* Die Nanking Road im Zentrum von Shanghai im Jahr 1930. *Photo: Getty Images*

12/13 Director Josef von Sternberg shooting *Shanghai Express* in 1932. *Le réalisateur Josef von Sternberg sur le tournage de Shanghai Express en 1932.* Der Filmregisseur Josef von Sternberg dreht 1932 den Film »Shanghai Express«. *Photo: Hulton Archive/Getty Images*

14/15 Bird's-eye view of Communist-era Shanghai. *Vue aérienne de Shanghai à l'époque communiste.* Shanghai in der kommunistischen Ära aus der Vogelperspektive. *Photo: Hulton Archive/Getty Images*

16/17 After the People's Revolution: entrance to Beijing's Forbidden City. *Après la révolution populaire ; entrée de la Cité interdite de Pékin.* Nach der Volksrevolution: Eingang zur Verbotenen Stadt in Peking. *Photo: Bettmann/CORBIS*

18/19 Pedicab drivers in Tiananmen Square, the "Place of Heavenly Peace." *Conducteurs de cyclopousse sur la place Tiananmen, la « place de la Paix céleste ».* Rikschafahrer am Tiananmen-Platz, dem »Platz des Himmlischen Friedens«. *Photo: Richard Harrington/Getty Images*

20/21 1977: view of Tiananmen Square and Chairman Mao's mausoleum. *Vue de la place Tiananmen et du mausolée de Mao en 1977.* 1977: Blick auf den Tiananmen-Platz und das Mausoleum des Großen Vorsitzenden Mao. *Photo: Keystone/Getty Images*

22/23 Cyclists on the road to a Ming tomb, near Beijing. *Cyclistes sur la route d'un tombeau Ming, près de Pékin.* Radfahrer auf der Straße zu einem Grab aus der Ming-Zeit, unweit von Peking. *Photo: Carl & Ann Purcell/CORBIS*

24/25 Still waters: rowboats at Beihai Park, Beijing. *Promenade en barque sur les eaux calmes du parc Beihai à Pékin.* Stille Wasser: Ruderboote im Beihai-Park, Peking. *Photo: Carl & Ann Purcell/CORBIS*

26/27 Barge on the historic Beijing-Hangzhou Grand Canal. *Péniche sur le Grand Canal Pékin-Hangzhou.* Lastkahn auf dem historischen Großen Kanal von Peking nach Hangzhou. *Photo: STR/AFP/Getty Images*

28/29 Graceful old bridges on the Grand Canal in Hangzhou. *Gracieuses silhouettes des vieux ponts du Grand Canal à Hangzhou.* Anmutige alte Brücken auf dem Großen Kanal in Hangzhou.

30/31 Long and legendary: the Great Wall of China. *La longue et mythique Grande Muraille de Chine.* Ebenso lang wie legendär: die Chinesische Mauer.

32/33 Climbing history: a walk along the Great Wall. *Promenade à travers l'histoire sur la Grande Muraille.* Ein Spaziergang durch die Geschichte auf der Chinesischen Mauer.

34/35 Pagoda in Jingshan Park, overlooking Beijing. *Pagode du parc Jingshan, sur les hauteurs de Pékin.* Pagode im Jing-Shan-Park mit Blick auf Peking.
Photo: China Photos/Getty Images

36/37 Dumpling soup, al fresco, on a Beijing street. *Dégustation d'une soupe de raviolis chinois dans une rue de Pékin.* Teigtaschensuppe unter freiem Himmel in einer Straße in Peking.
Photo: Peter Parks/AFP/Getty Images

38/39 Chinese police patrol Tiananmen Square, 2005. *Patrouille de police chinoise place Tiananmen, 2005.* Die chinesische Polizei patrouilliert auf dem Tiananmen-Platz, 2005.
Photo: Cancan Chu/Getty Images

40/41 A restored Qing Dynasty house, Beijing. *Maison restaurée de l'époque de la dynastie Qing, Pékin.* Ein restauriertes Haus der Qing-Dynastie in Peking.

42/43 The Sichuan Pavilion at Beijing's China Club. *Le pavillon Sichuan du China Club de Pékin.* Der Sichuan-Pavillon im China Club von Peking.

44/45 In the traditional courtyard of the China Club. *Dans la cour traditionnelle du China Club.* Im traditionellen Innenhof des China Club.

46/47 An entrance gate in the Forbidden City, Beijing. *Une porte de la Cité interdite, Pékin.* Ein Eingangstor in der Verbotenen Stadt, Peking.

48/49 Lantern Festival in Chengdu, Sichuan province. *Festival des lanternes à Chengdu, province du Sichuan.* Laternenfest in Chengdu in der Provinz Sichuan.
Photo: China Photos/Getty Images

50/51 New and bold: the glitzy skyscrapers of Pudong, Shanghai. *Audace de la nouveauté : les éblouissants gratte-ciel de Pudong, à Shanghai.* Neu und verwegen: Die glitzernden Wolkenkratzer von Pudong, Shanghai.

52/53 Hong Kong's magnificent harbor and skyline dazzles by night. *Vue de nuit sur le magnifique port de Hong Kong et la silhouette des gratte-ciel.* Hongkongs prunkvoller Hafen mit seiner funkelnden Skyline bei Nacht.

54/55 A vintage limousine parked outside the Red Capital Club, Beijing. *Limousine d'époque devant le Red Capital Club, Pékin.* Ein Oldtimer parkt vor dem Red Capital Club in Peking.

"Golden orioles flit across the beams,
Purple doves descend from lattice screens.
Myself, I think I've found a place that suits."

In Abbot Zan's Room in Daiyu Temple, Du Fu

«Des loriots dorés volettent entre les poutres,
Des colombes pourpres descendent des paravents.
Personnellement, je pense avoir trouvé ma place.»

Dans la chambre de l'abbé Zan au temple de Daiyu, Du Fu

»Wo Goldpirole über Sparren ziehn
und Purpurtauben vorm Fenster fliehn,
dort fand ich den mir genehmen Ort.«

Im Zimmer von Abt Zan im Daiyu-Tempel, Du Fu

INTERIORS

Intérieurs   Einsichten

60/61 Shanghai retro: Art Deco tinted-glass doors in Hong Kong's China Club. *Style rétro : portes vitrées Art Déco au China Club de Hong Kong.* Shanghai im Retro-Look: Glastüren im Art-Deco-Stil in Hongkongs China Club.

62/63 Tea at the China Club's "Long March Bar," Hong Kong. *Thé au « Bar de la Longue Marche » du China Club de Hong Kong.* Tee in der »Langen-Marsch-Bar« im China Club, Hongkong.

64/65 The main dining room at the China Club, Hong Kong. *Salle à manger principale du China Club de Hong Kong.* Der große Speisesaal im China Club, Hongkong.

66/67 Twin lions guard the courtyard at Beijing's China Club. *Deux lions montent la garde dans la cour du China Club de Pékin.* Ein Löwenpaar bewacht den Innenhof des China Club in Peking.

68/69 A Ming period private dining room, China Club, Beijing. *Salle à manger privée de l'époque Ming, China Club de Pékin.* Ein privates Esszimmer aus der Ming-Zeit im China Club, Peking.

70/71 Another Ming period dining room, China Club. *Autre salle à manger privée de la période Ming, au China Club.* Ein weiteres Esszimmer aus der Ming-Zeit im China Club.

72/73 Raise the red lantern: a guest suite in the China Club. *La lanterne rouge resplendit : une suite du China Club.* »Die rote Laterne«: Gästesuite im China Club.

74/75 Afternoon tea and silk brocade, in a China Club suite. *Brocarts de soie à l'heure du thé, dans une suite du China Club.* Nachmittagstee und Seidenbrokat in einer Suite des China Club.

76/77 Red window frames in the 17th-century. Beijing house of Jehanne de Biolley. *Encadre-ments de fenêtres rouges dans la maison pékinoise du XVIIᵉ siècle de Jehanne de Biolley.* Rote Fensterrahmen in Jehanne de Biolleys Pekinger Wohnsitz aus dem 17. Jh.

78/79 Red lacquer and green leather: de Biolley's living room. *Laque rouge et cuir vert : le salon de Jehanne de Biolley.* Roter Lack und grünes Leder: Das Wohnzimmer von Jehanne de Biolley.

80/81 Wooden columns give de Biolley's living room a ceremonial feel. *Les colonnes de bois donnent une touche solennelle au salon de Jehanne de Biolley.* Holzsäulen verleihen dem Wohnzimmer von Jehanne de Biolley ein feierliches Flair.

82/83 Sumptuous silks and velvets adorn de Biolley's bronze bed. *De sompteuses étoffes de soie et de velours ornent le lit de bronze de Jehanne de Biolley.* Üppige Seiden- und Samtstoffe schmücken das de-Biolley'sche Bronzebett.

84/85 Shanghai modern: the luxe, Asian-inspired rooms at Grand Hyatt hotel. *Shanghai moderne : luxueuses chambres d'inspiration asiatique de l'hôtel Grand Hyatt.* Modernes Shanghai: Purer Luxus in den asiatisch inspirierten Räumen des Grand-Hyatt-Hotels.

86/87 Sky dining: sweeping view from the Jin Mao Club, Grand Hyatt. *Dîner en plein ciel : vue panoramique depuis le Jin Mao Club, hôtel Grand Hyatt.* »Sky dining«: Panoramablick aus dem Jin-Mao-Club des Grand-Hyatt-Hotels.

88/89 Japanese architect Shigeru Ban's Furniture House, near Beijing. *Maison de l'architecte japonais Shigeru Ban, près de Pékin.* Das »Furniture House« des japanischen Architekten Shigeru Ban, unweit von Peking.

90/91 Inside Kengo Kuma's Bamboo Wall House, near Beijing. *Intérieur de la maison de bambou de Kengo Kuma, près de Pékin.* Wechselnde Perspektiven: Im Innern von Kengo Kumas Haus »Bamboo Wall«, unweit von Peking.

92/93 Rugged vista: moveable bamboo walls reveal the natural landscape. *Nature sauvage : les cloisons mobiles en bambou révèlent le paysage extérieur.* Verschiebbare Bambuswände geben den Blick auf die Landschaft frei.

94/95 Warm wood: traditional bed in Pascale Desvaux's Beijing living room. *Chaleur du bois : lit traditionnel dans le salon de Pascale Desvaux à Pékin.* Warmes Holz: Ein traditionelles Bett im Wohnzimmer von Pascale Desvaux, Peking.

96/97 Circular Chinese moon gates are Desvaux's repeating motif. *Les portes-lune chinoises sont un motif récurrent chez Pascale Desvaux.* Kreisförmige chinesische Mondtore sind ein beliebtes Motiv bei Pascale Desvaux.

98/99 Blue moon: a round portal leads to the kitchen. *Lune bleue : une porte ronde mène à la cuisine.* Blauer Mond: Ein runder Mauerdurchbruch führt in die Küche.

100/101 Replica of Chairman Mao's study, in Beijing's Red Capital Residence. *Réplique du bureau du Grand Timonier dans l'hôtel Red Capital Residence, à Pékin.* Nachbau des Arbeitszimmers des Großen Vorsitzenden Mao in Pekings Red Capital Residence.

102/103 Shanghai comfort: Pia Pierre's renovated French Concession House. *Grand confort de la maison rénovée de Pia Pierre dans l'ancienne Concession française de Shanghai.* Gemütlichkeit à la Shanghai: Das renovierte Haus von Pia Pierre in der Französischen Konzession.

104/105 Inside Pierre's Shanghai study, two 18th-century elmwood chairs. *Deux fauteuils en orme du XVIIIe siècle dans le bureau de Pia Pierre.* Zwei Ulmenholzstühle aus dem 18. Jh. im Shanghai-Atelier von Pia Pierre.

106/107 Hanging scrolls add tradition and warmth to Pierre's living room. *Des rouleaux suspendus apportent une touche de tradition et de chaleur au salon de Pia Pierre.* Schriftrollen bringen Tradition und Wärme in das Pierre'sche Wohnzimmer.

108/109 In the Pierre house: modern Chinese art and exposed brick. *Dans la maison de Pia Pierre : art moderne chinois et brique nue.* Im Innern des Pierre'schen Hauses: Moderne chinesische Kunst und rohe Ziegelwände.

110/111 Casual modern decor in Leonardo Griglie's Qing-era house, Beijing. *Décor moderne et sobre dans la résidence d'époque Qing de Leonardo Griglie, à Pékin.* Lässiger moderner Dekor im aus der Qing-Zeit stammenden Haus von Leonardo Griglie, Peking.

112/113 Sung Dynasty-inspired tea lounge, at Leonardo Griglie's house. *Salon de thé décoré dans l'esprit de la dynastie Sung, dans la maison de Leonardo Griglie.* Ein von der Sung-Dynastie inspirierter Teesaal im Haus von Leonardo Griglie.

114/115 Dining at Fuchun Resort: lacquered plates and linen napkins. *Dîner au Fuchun Resort : assiettes laquées et serviettes en lin.* Abendessen im Fuchun Resort: Lackteller und Leinenservietten.

116/117 Hangzhou luxe: villas at Fuchun Resort have private pools. *Hangzhou et le luxe : les villas du Fuchun Resort sont équipées de piscines privées.* Hangzhou-Luxus: Die Villen im Fuchun Resort haben private Swimmingpools.

118/119 Light upon still water: another Fuchun Resort pool. *Jeux de lumière sur l'eau calme : une autre piscine du Fuchun Resort.* Lichtreflexe auf dem Wasser: Ein weiterer Pool des Fuchun Resorts.

120/121 Yellow pillows accentuate Sandra and Yan d'Auriol's Hong Kong house. *Des coussins jaunes illuminent la maison de Sandra et Yan d'Auriol à Hong Kong.* Gelbe Kissen setzen im Hongkonger Haus von Sandra und Yan d'Auriol farbige Akzente.

122/123 Mirror, mirror: reflections in a Chinese glass, d'Auriol house. *Miroir, mon beau miroir : reflet chinois chez les d'Auriol.* Spieglein, Spieglein: Spiegeleffekte im Haus der d'Auriols.

"... All difficult things have their origin in that which is easy, and great things in that which is small..."

Lao Tzu, *Chinese philosopher*

«... Toutes les choses difficiles trouvent leur origine dans ce qui est simple et toutes les grandes choses dans ce qui est petit...»

Lao Tzu, *philosophe chinois*

«... Alles Schwere auf Erden beginnt stets als Leichtes und alles Große auf Erden beginnt stets als Kleines...»

Lao Tzu, *chinesischer Philosoph*

DETAILS

Détails   Details

东方红 毛泽东画典

中国文联出版公司

子高级修养学堂

冬季特价
2004年1月1日 – 2004年2月29日

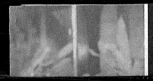

TANDOOR
INDIAN CUISINE

怡泉·园
FAIRVIEW GARDEN
BEIJING·北京

TANDOOR
INDIAN CUISINE

冬季特价
2004年1月1日 – 2004年2月29日
标准间 人民币 240 元

TRANQ

阿凡提娱乐传媒集团
A Fun Ti Omni Media Group
A Fun Ti
Hometown Music Restaurant
阿凡提

阿凡提娱乐传媒集团
A Fun Ti Entertainment Media Group
阿凡提
家乡音乐餐厅
A Fun Ti

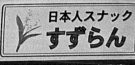

阿凡提娱乐传媒集团
A Fun Ti Entertainment Media Group
阿凡提
家乡音乐餐厅

日本人スナック
すずらん
明朗会計で安心できる店

that's
Beijing

VISTA CLINIC
维世达诊所

锦都久缘餐厅
Capital Garden

阿凡提娱乐传媒集团
A Fun Ti Omni Media Group
A Fun Ti
Hometown Music Restaurant
阿凡提
家乡音乐餐厅

锦都久缘餐厅
Capital Garden

阿凡提娱乐传媒集团
A Fun Ti Omni Media Group
A Fun Ti

泽东像章图谱

于安廷 主编

毛主席和他的亲密战友
林彪同志检阅文化
革命大军

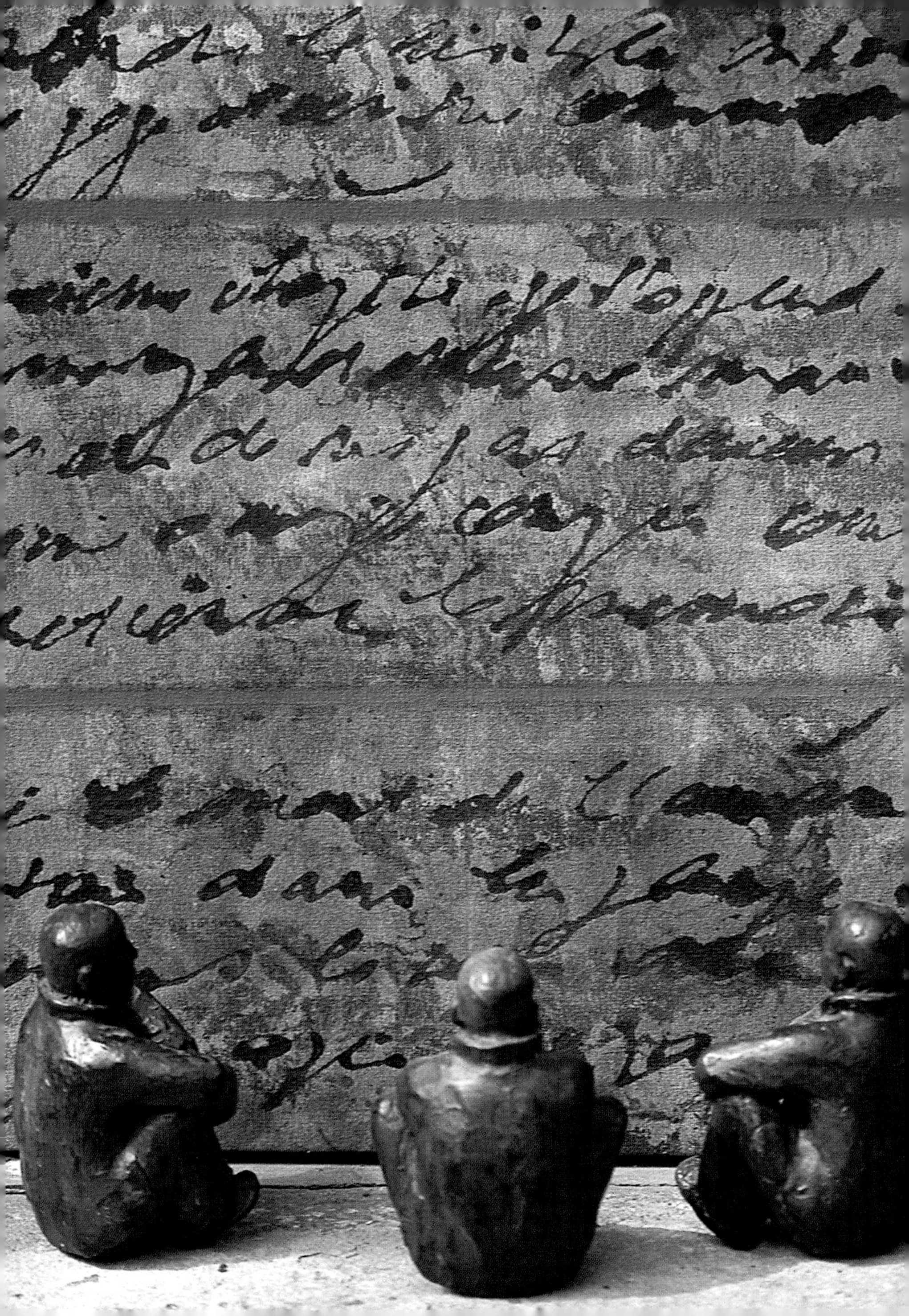

131 At Red Capital Residence: A uniformed staff member greets guests. *Au Red Capital Residence, un membre du personnel en uniforme accueille la clientéle.* In der Red Capital Residence: Eine Hotelangestellte in Uniform begrüßt Gäste.

132 Mao's image at the entrance to Beijing's Forbidden City. *Portrait de Mao à l'entrée de la Cité interdite de Pékin.* Maos Konterfei am Eingang zur Verbotenen Stadt in Peking.

133 "The East Is Red": a revolutionary book at Red Capital Residence. *L'Orient est rouge : livre révolutionnaire au Red Capital Residence.* »Der Osten ist rot«: Ein Buch aus der Revolutionszeit in der Red Capital Residence.

134 Dazzling detail: Qing-dynasty roof designs at Leonardo Griglie's residence. *Beauté du détail : motifs des toits de l'époque Qing chez Leonardo Griglie.* Ein verblüffendes Detail: Dachverzierungen der Qing-Dynastie im Haus von Leonardo Griglie.

136 Antique birdcage, Pascale Desvaux house, Beijing. *Cage ancienne à oiseaux, chez Pascale Desvaux à Pékin.* Ein antiker Vogelkäfig im Haus von Pascale Desvaux, Peking.

137 In Desvaux house: characters on Chinese lanterns say "Blessings." *Chez Pascale Desvaux : les caractères sur les lanternes chinoises signifient « bénédictions ».* Im Haus von Pascale Desvaux: Chinesische Segenswünsche auf einer Laterne.

139 Also in Desvaux house: chairs dating from the Cultural Revolution. *Toujours chez Pascale Desvaux : fauteuils datant de la Révolution culturelle.* Ebenfalls im Haus von Pascale Desvaux: Stühle aus der Zeit der Kulturrevolution.

140 Ceramic statue entwined with handmade jewelry by Jehanne de Biolley. *Statue en céramique décorée de bijoux fabriqués par Jehanne de Biolley.* Eine Keramikstatue mit handgearbeitetem Schmuck von Jehanne de Biolley.

141 Jehanne de Biolley's necklace made from blue and red Chinese seeds. *Collier de Jehanne de Biolley, réalisé avec des graines chinoises bleues et rouges.* Jehanne de Biolley's Kette aus blauen und roten chinesischen Samenkörnern.

143 Songbirds bring music to Leonardo Griglie's Beijing courtyard. *Le chant des oiseaux emplit la cour intérieure de la résidence de Leonardo Griglie à Pékin.* Vögel bringen Musik in Leonardo Griglies Innenhof in Peking.

144 Dancing dragons adorn a facade at the Griglie residence. *Des dragons dansants ornent une façade de la résidence de Leonardo Griglie.* Tanzende Drachen schmücken eine Fassade des Griglie-Wohnsitzes.

145 Silk print on a Chinese lantern, Desvaux house. *Soie imprimée sur une lanterne chinoise, chez Pascale Desvaux.* Seidendruck auf einer chinesischen Laterne im Haus von Pascale Desvaux.

146 Far East romance: a concubine's bed in Red Capital Residence. *Romance d'Extrême-Orient : lit de concubine au Red Capital Residence.* Fernost-Romantik: Das Bett einer Konkubine in der Red Capital Residence.

148 Ceramic vases and lacquered boxes, at de Biolley house. *Vases en céramique et boîtes laquées chez Jehanne de Biolley.* Keramikvasen und Lacktruhen im Haus von Jehanne de Biolley.

149 The luxurious, canopied bed in the de Biolley home. *Le splendide lit à baldaquin de Jehanne de Biolley.* Das luxuriöse Himmelbett von Jehanne de Biolley.

151 China's red star flag adorns the table napkins at Beijing's China Club. *Serviettes de table décorées de l'étoile rouge au China Club de Pékin.* Chinas roter Stern ziert die Servietten im China Club von Peking.

152 The China Club's bright green ceramic plates and bowls. *Assiettes et bols en céramique vert vif au China Club.* Hellgrüne Keramikteller und Schalen im China Club.

153 Mao-era ceramic kitsch at Red Capital Residence. *Céramique kitsch de l'époque de Mao au Red Capital Residence.* Porzellankitsch aus der Mao-Zeit in der Red Capital Residence.

154 Cutouts of 1970's-era Mao Zedong portraits, Griglie house. *Collage de portraits de Mao Zedong dans les années 1970, chez Leonardo Griglie.* Porträtausschnitte von Mao Zedong aus den 1970er-Jahren im Haus von Leonardo Griglie.

156 Bright entrance: lantern at Beijing's China Club. *Entrée en lumière : lanterne du China Club de Pékin.* Strahlender Eingang: Eine Laterne im China Club von Peking.

157 A welcome to the Red Capital Residence in Beijing. *Bienvenue au Red Capital Residence de Pékin.* Willkommen in der Red Capital Residence in Peking.

158 Old gramophone at de Biolley house. *Vieux gramophone chez Jehanne de Biolley.* Ein altes Grammophon im Haus von Jehanne de Biolley.

160 Lions guard the entrances to the Forbidden City. *Des lions montent la garde à l'entrée de la Cité interdite.* Löwen bewachen den Eingang zur Verbotenen Stadt.

161 Business cards on display at the Beijing China Club. *Cartes de visite à l'entrée du China Club de Pékin.* Visitenkarten im China Club von Peking.

162 Red earth: fire emergency tools at Pascale Desvaux's house. Beijing. *Terre rouge : outils de la effacement chez Pascale Desvaux à Pékin.* Rote Erde: Löschwerkzeuge im Haus von Pascale Desvaux, Peking.

164 Breakfast at Red Capital Residence, Beijing. *Petit-déjeuner au Red Capital Residence de Pékin.* Frühstück in der Red Capital Residence, Peking.

165 Mao memorabilia at Red Capital Residence. *Souvenir de Mao au Red Capital Residence.* Mao-Devotionalien in der Red Capital Residence.

167 An ashtray commemorates the Cultural Revolution at Red Capital Residence. *Cendrier commémorant la Révolution culturelle au Red Capital Residence.* Ein Aschenbecher in der Red Capital Residence erinnert an die Kulturrevolution.

168 A little visitor hides under a lion guardian statue, Forbidden City. *Un petit visiteur se cache sous la statue d'un des lions gardant la Cité interdite.* Ein kleiner Besucher versteckt sich unter einer Löwenstatue in der Verbotenen Stadt.

169 Serene Buddha at Fuchun Resort, Hangzhou. *Bouddha serein au Fuchun Resort de Hangzhou.* Ein heiterer Buddha im Fuchun Resort, Hangzhou.

171 Pedicab driver at Red Capital Residence. *Conducteur de cyclopousse au Red Capital Residence.* Rikschafahrer in der Red Capital Residence.

172 Metal lanterns at Fuchun Resort, Hangzhou. *Lanternes en métal au Fuchun Resort de Hangzhou.* Metalllaternen im Fuchun Resort, Hangzhou.

173 Hangzhou tea served at Fuchun Resort. *Thé de Hangzhou servi au Fuchun Resort.* Hangzhou-Tee im Fuchun Resort.

174 Detail, Pascale Desvaux house, Beijing. *Détail, maison de Pascale Desvaux, Pékin.* Ein Detail aus Pascale Desvauxs Haus in Peking.

176/177 Antique birdcages in Pascale Desvaux house, Beijing. *Cages à oiseaux anciennes, chez Pascale Desvaux à Pékin.* Antike Vogelkäfige im Haus von Pascale Desvaux, Peking.

179 Portrait of young Chairman Mao, Griglie house. *Portrait du jeune Mao, chez Leonardo Griglie.* Porträt des jungen Großen Vorsitzenden Mao im Haus von Leonardo Griglie.

180 A soldier's salute: near the entrance to China Club, Beijing. *Salut militaire, à l'entrée du China Club de Pékin.* »Soldatengruß« am Eingang des China Clubs, Peking.

181 Lion brass ring pull, Red Capital Residence, Beijing. *Heurtoir en bronze à tête de lion, Red Capital Residence, Pékin.* Löwen-Messingklopfer in der Red Capital Residence, Peking.

183 The Clubhouse Lounge, Fuchun Resort, Hangzhou. *Salon du club-house au Fuchun Resort de Hangzhou.* Die Clubhouse Lounge im Fuchun Reort, Hangzhou.

184 Entrance hallway at Pia Pierre's Shanghai house. *Entrée de la maison de Pia Pierre à Shanghai.* Hausflur von Pia Pierre in Shanghai.

185 Calligraphy-decorated headboard at Grand Hyatt, Shanghai. *Tête de lit ornée de calligraphies à l'hôtel Grand Hyatt de Shanghai.* Ein mit Kalligraphien geschmücktes Kopfende im Grand-Hyatt-Hotel, Shanghai.

186 The Clubhouse Lounge, Fuchun Resort, Hangzhou. *Statue de Bouddha au Fuchun Resort de Hangzhou.* Buddha-statue im Fuchun Resort, Hangzhou.

Addresses

RED CAPITAL RESIDENCE
No. 67 Dongsi Batiao
Dongcheng District
Beijing 100007
tel: +86 (10) 640 27 150
email: info@redcapitalclub.com.cn
www.redcaptialclub.com.cn

THE CHINA CLUB BEIJING
No. 51 Xi Rong Xian Lane
Xi Dan Beijing 100031
tel: +86 (10) 660 58 435
fax: +86 (10) 660 39 594
email: tccbmem@public.bta.net.cn

GRAND HYATT SHANGHAI
Jin Mao Tower
88 Century Boulevard Pudong
Shanghai 2001121
tel: +86 (21) 504 91 234
fax: +86 (21) 504 91 111
email: info@hyattshanghai.com
www.shanghai.grand.hyatt.com

THE CHINA CLUB HONG KONG
Clarence Chan
13/F The Old Bank of China Building
Bank Street
Central Hong Kong
tel: + 85 (2) 284 00 233
fax: + 85 (2) 252 28 011
email: tccgm01@netvigator.com

FUCHUN RESORT
Fuyang Section
Hangfu Yanjiang Road
Zhejiang 311401
tel: +86 (571) 634 61 111
fax: +86 (571) 634 61 222
email: fuchunresort@lcpc.biz

The Hotel Book. Great Escapes Asia Christiane Reiter / Ed. Angelika Taschen / Hardcover, 400 pp. / € 29.99 / $ 39.99 / £ 19.99 / ¥ 5.900

Inside Asia Photos Reto Guntli / Ed. Angelika Taschen / Sunil Sethi / Hardcover, 2 volumes 880 pp. / € 99.99 / $ 125 / £ 69.99 / ¥ 15.000

"Be it a monastery in Tibet, a coffee plantation in Java or a designer house in Japan – Inside Asia reveals the diversity of this continent." —*ELLE*, Munich on *Inside Asia*

"Buy them all and add some pleasure to your life."

African Style
Ed. Angelika Taschen

Alchemy & Mysticism
Alexander Roob

All-American Ads 40ˢ
Ed. Jim Heimann

All-American Ads 50ˢ
Ed. Jim Heimann

All-American Ads 60ˢ
Ed. Jim Heimann

American Indian
Dr. Sonja Schierle

Angels
Gilles Néret

Architecture Now!
Ed. Philip Jodidio

Art Now
Eds. Burkhard Riemschneider, Uta Grosenick

Atget's Paris
Ed. Hans Christian Adam

Berlin Style
Ed. Angelika Taschen

Cars of the 50s
Ed. Jim Heimann, Tony Thacker

Cars of the 60s
Ed. Jim Heimann, Tony Thacker

Cars of the 70s
Ed. Jim Heimann, Tony Thacker

Chairs
Charlotte & Peter Fiell

Christmas
Ed. Jim Heimann, Steven Heller

Classic Rock Covers
Ed. Michael Ochs

Design Handbook
Charlotte & Peter Fiell

Design of the 20ᵗʰ Century
Charlotte & Peter Fiell

Design for the 21ˢᵗ Century
Charlotte & Peter Fiell

Devils
Gilles Néret

Digital Beauties
Ed. Julius Wiedemann

Robert Doisneau
Ed. Jean-Claude Gautrand

East German Design
Ralf Ulrich / Photos: Ernst Hedler

Egypt Style
Ed. Angelika Taschen

Encyclopaedia Anatomica
Ed. Museo La Specola Florence

M.C. Escher

Fashion
Ed. The Kyoto Costume Institute

Fashion Now!
Ed. Terry Jones, Susie Rushton

Fruit
Ed. George Brookshaw, Uta Pellgrü-Gagel

HR Giger
HR Giger

Grand Tour
Harry Seidler

Graphic Design
Eds. Charlotte & Peter Fiell

Greece Style
Ed. Angelika Taschen

Halloween
Ed. Jim Heimann, Steven Heller

Havana Style
Ed. Angelika Taschen

Homo Art
Gilles Néret

Hot Rods
Ed. Coco Shinomiya, Tony Thacker

Hula
Ed. Jim Heimann

Indian Style
Ed. Angelika Taschen

India Bazaar
Samantha Harrison, Bari Kumar

Industrial Design
Charlotte & Peter Fiell

Japanese Beauties
Ed. Alex Gross

Krazy Kids' Food
Eds. Steve Roden, Dan Goodsell

Las Vegas
Ed. Jim Heimann, W. R. Wilkerson III

London Style
Ed. Angelika Taschen

Mexicana
Ed. Jim Heimann

Mexico Style
Ed. Angelika Taschen

Morocco Style
Ed. Angelika Taschen

New York Style
Ed. Angelika Taschen

Paris Style
Ed. Angelika Taschen

Penguin
Frans Lanting

20ᵗʰ Century Photography
Museum Ludwig Cologne

Photo Icons I
Hans-Michael Koetzle

Photo Icons II
Hans-Michael Koetzle

Pierre et Gilles
Eric Troncy

Provence Style
Ed. Angelika Taschen

Robots & Spaceships
Ed. Teruhisa Kitahara

Safari Style
Ed. Angelika Taschen

Seaside Style
Ed. Angelika Taschen

Albertus Seba. Butterflies
Irmgard Müsch

Albertus Seba. Shells & Corals
Irmgard Müsch

Signs
Ed. Julius Wiedemann

South African Style
Ed. Angelika Taschen

Starck
Philippe Starck

Surfing
Ed. Jim Heimann

Sweden Style
Ed. Angelika Taschen

Sydney Style
Ed. Angelika Taschen

Tattoos
Ed. Henk Schiffmacher

Tiffany
Jacob Baal-Teshuva

Tiki Style
Sven Kirsten

Tuscany Style
Ed. Angelika Taschen

Valentines
Ed. Jim Heimann, Steven Heller

Web Design: Best Studios
Ed. Julius Wiedemann

Web Design: Flash Sites
Ed. Julius Wiedemann

Web Design: Portfolios
Ed. Julius Wiedemann

Women Artists in the 20ᵗʰ and 21ˢᵗ Century
Ed. Uta Grosenick